EMMANUEL JOSEPH

From Silicon Dreams to Concrete Realities, The Strategies of Business Moguls

Copyright © 2025 by Emmanuel Joseph

All rights reserved. No part of this publication may be reproduced, stored or transmitted in any form or by any means, electronic, mechanical, photocopying, recording, scanning, or otherwise without written permission from the publisher. It is illegal to copy this book, post it to a website, or distribute it by any other means without permission.

First edition

This book was professionally typeset on Reedsy.
Find out more at reedsy.com

Contents

1	Chapter 1: The Visionaries	1
2	Chapter 2: The Power of Perseverance	3
3	Chapter 3: Building a Strong Team	5
4	Chapter 4: Innovation and Adaptation	7
5	Chapter 5: Strategic Planning	9
6	Chapter 6: Financial Acumen	11
7	Chapter 7: Effective Marketing	13
8	Chapter 8: Customer-Centric Approach	15
9	Chapter 9: Leveraging Technology	17
10	Chapter 10: Ethical Leadership	19
11	Chapter 11: Global Expansion	21
12	Chapter 12: Leaving a Legacy	23

1

Chapter 1: The Visionaries

Business moguls often start with a vision, a dream that propels them into uncharted territories. These individuals possess an extraordinary ability to see potential where others see obstacles. They have a knack for identifying gaps in the market and devising innovative solutions to fill those gaps. Visionaries are not deterred by the unknown; instead, they are motivated by the possibilities that lie ahead. Their dreams are the seeds from which their empires grow, nurtured by a relentless pursuit of their goals.

In the early stages, visionaries are often met with skepticism. Their ideas may seem far-fetched or impractical to those around them. However, their unwavering belief in their vision drives them forward. They spend countless hours researching, planning, and refining their ideas. This chapter delves into the mindset of visionaries, exploring how they cultivate their dreams and transform them into viable business concepts.

A key aspect of being a visionary is the ability to inspire others. Business moguls must communicate their vision effectively, rallying support from investors, partners, and employees. They paint a vivid picture of the future they envision, instilling confidence and excitement in those around them. This chapter highlights the importance of storytelling and persuasive communication in turning dreams into concrete realities.

Another crucial element is risk-taking. Visionaries are willing to take calculated risks to bring their ideas to life. They understand that failure is a part of the journey and view setbacks as opportunities to learn and grow. This chapter examines the role of risk-taking in the success of business moguls, emphasizing the need for resilience and adaptability.

Finally, this chapter explores the long-term thinking that defines visionaries. They are not focused on short-term gains but rather on creating lasting impact. Their vision extends beyond immediate success, aiming for sustainable growth and legacy. This forward-thinking approach sets the foundation for their business ventures and guides their strategic decisions.

2

Chapter 2: The Power of Perseverance

Perseverance is a fundamental quality that sets business moguls apart from others. The journey to success is fraught with challenges and setbacks, but moguls possess an unyielding determination to overcome them. This chapter delves into the significance of perseverance in the lives of successful business leaders, highlighting how their unwavering commitment drives them forward.

Setbacks are inevitable in any entrepreneurial journey. Business moguls encounter numerous obstacles, from financial difficulties to market resistance. However, their ability to persist in the face of adversity is what ultimately sets them apart. This chapter explores how moguls develop resilience and use failures as stepping stones to success.

Perseverance also involves a continuous pursuit of improvement. Business moguls are never satisfied with the status quo; they are always seeking ways to enhance their products, services, and operations. This chapter examines the importance of a growth mindset and the willingness to adapt and evolve in a rapidly changing business landscape.

Support systems play a crucial role in fostering perseverance. Behind every successful mogul is a network of mentors, advisors, and supporters who provide guidance and encouragement. This chapter explores the significance of building a strong support system and how it contributes to the resilience and determination of business leaders.

Lastly, this chapter highlights the importance of maintaining a positive attitude. Optimism and a can-do spirit are essential for persevering through tough times. Business moguls approach challenges with a problem-solving mindset, viewing obstacles as opportunities to innovate and excel. This chapter delves into the psychological aspects of perseverance and how a positive outlook can fuel success.

3

Chapter 3: Building a Strong Team

No business mogul achieves success alone; behind every great leader is a talented and dedicated team. This chapter focuses on the importance of building a cohesive and high-performing team, highlighting the strategies used by business moguls to attract, retain, and motivate top talent.

The foundation of a strong team is trust and alignment with the company's vision. Business moguls prioritize creating a culture of trust and transparency, where team members feel valued and empowered. This chapter explores the principles of effective leadership and how moguls foster a sense of belonging and purpose within their teams.

Recruiting the right people is a critical aspect of team building. Business moguls have a keen eye for talent and understand the importance of hiring individuals who not only possess the necessary skills but also align with the company's values and culture. This chapter delves into the recruitment process, from identifying talent to conducting interviews and making hiring decisions.

Once a strong team is in place, effective communication is key to ensuring collaboration and productivity. Business moguls implement communication strategies that facilitate open dialogue, feedback, and idea-sharing. This chapter examines the various communication tools and practices used by moguls to keep their teams connected and engaged.

Finally, this chapter explores the significance of continuous learning and development. Business moguls invest in the growth of their team members, providing opportunities for training, mentorship, and professional development. This chapter highlights the importance of nurturing talent and creating a culture of continuous improvement within the organization.

4

Chapter 4: Innovation and Adaptation

Innovation and adaptation are essential for staying competitive in a rapidly evolving business landscape. Business moguls are not afraid to take risks and embrace change, constantly seeking new ways to improve and innovate. This chapter examines how moguls foster a culture of innovation within their organizations and adapt to industry trends.

Fostering innovation begins with creating an environment that encourages creativity and experimentation. Business moguls promote a culture where new ideas are welcomed, and employees are encouraged to think outside the box. This chapter explores the various strategies used by moguls to inspire innovation, from brainstorming sessions to innovation labs.

Adaptation is equally important in the face of changing market conditions. Business moguls are agile and responsive, quickly pivoting their strategies to stay ahead of the competition. This chapter examines the importance of staying informed about industry trends and being willing to make bold moves when necessary.

Risk-taking is a crucial element of innovation. Business moguls understand that taking calculated risks is essential for achieving breakthroughs. This chapter delves into the mindset of risk-taking and how moguls evaluate potential risks and rewards to make informed decisions.

Collaboration is another key aspect of innovation. Business moguls recognize the value of diverse perspectives and encourage cross-functional collaboration within their organizations. This chapter explores how moguls create opportunities for teams to collaborate and share ideas, leading to innovative solutions.

Lastly, this chapter highlights the importance of continuous learning and staying curious. Business moguls are lifelong learners who seek out new knowledge and insights to stay ahead of the curve. This chapter examines how moguls invest in their own learning and encourage a culture of curiosity within their organizations.

5

Chapter 5: Strategic Planning

Strategic planning is the backbone of any successful business venture. Business moguls are meticulous planners who set clear goals and devise strategies to achieve them. This chapter delves into the importance of strategic planning, the process of setting achievable milestones, and the methods used to track progress and make adjustments along the way.

The foundation of strategic planning is setting a clear vision and mission for the organization. Business moguls articulate their long-term goals and ensure that their strategies align with their overall vision. This chapter explores the process of defining a vision and mission and how it guides strategic decision-making.

Setting specific, measurable, achievable, relevant, and time-bound (SMART) goals is a crucial aspect of strategic planning. Business moguls break down their long-term vision into actionable steps and set milestones to track progress. This chapter examines the importance of goal-setting and how moguls use SMART criteria to create effective plans.

Resource allocation is another key element of strategic planning. Business moguls allocate resources, including time, money, and personnel, to ensure that their strategies are effectively implemented. This chapter delves into the process of resource allocation and how moguls prioritize tasks and initiatives to maximize efficiency and impact.

Monitoring and evaluation are essential for tracking progress and making necessary adjustments. Business moguls implement systems to measure performance, gather feedback, and analyze results. This chapter explores the various tools and techniques used by moguls to monitor progress and make data-driven decisions.

Finally, this chapter highlights the importance of flexibility and adaptability in strategic planning. Business moguls understand that plans may need to change in response to new information or shifting market conditions. This chapter examines how moguls remain agile and adjust their strategies to stay on course and achieve their goals.

6

Chapter 6: Financial Acumen

Understanding the financial aspects of running a business is essential for any mogul. This chapter explores the financial strategies employed by successful business leaders, including managing cash flow, securing funding, and making sound investments. It also highlights the importance of financial literacy and the role it plays in sustainable growth.

Managing cash flow is a critical aspect of financial acumen. Business moguls ensure that their businesses have sufficient liquidity to cover expenses and invest in growth opportunities. This chapter delves into the principles of cash flow management, including budgeting, forecasting, and optimizing working capital.

Securing funding is often a necessary step for business growth. Business moguls explore various funding options, from bootstrapping and loans to venture capital and public offerings. This chapter examines the different sources of funding and the strategies moguls use to attract investors and secure financing.

Sound investment decisions are crucial for maximizing returns and ensuring long-term sustainability. Business moguls carefully evaluate investment opportunities, considering factors such as risk, return, and alignment with their overall strategy. This chapter explores the principles of investment decision-making and how moguls build diversified portfolios to manage risk.

Financial literacy is the foundation of financial acumen. Business moguls prioritize understanding financial statements, key performance indicators, and economic trends. This chapter highlights the importance of financial education and how moguls use financial data to make informed decisions and drive business success.

Lastly, this chapter explores the role of financial technology (FinTech) in modern business. Business moguls leverage FinTech solutions to streamline financial operations, enhance efficiency, and gain valuable systems. This chapter highlights how moguls utilize financial technology to gain insights and stay competitive in the digital age.

7

Chapter 7: Effective Marketing

Marketing is the bridge that connects a business to its customers. Business moguls excel at creating compelling marketing campaigns that resonate with their target audience. This chapter discusses the various marketing techniques they use, from traditional advertising to digital marketing, and the importance of building a strong brand identity.

Effective marketing starts with understanding the customer. Business moguls invest in market research to identify their target audience's needs, preferences, and behaviors. This chapter explores the methods used to gather customer insights and how these insights inform marketing strategies.

Branding is a critical component of marketing. Business moguls focus on creating a strong brand identity that reflects the company's values and mission. This chapter delves into the elements of branding, including brand messaging, visual identity, and the creation of a memorable brand experience.

Digital marketing has become an essential tool for reaching customers in the modern age. Business moguls leverage digital platforms such as social media, email marketing, and search engine optimization to connect with their audience. This chapter examines the strategies used to create effective digital marketing campaigns and the importance of measuring and analyzing their impact.

Traditional marketing techniques still hold value in certain contexts. Business moguls utilize methods such as print advertising, television commercials, and event marketing to reach specific audiences. This chapter explores the benefits of traditional marketing and how it can complement digital efforts.

Lastly, this chapter highlights the importance of customer engagement and loyalty. Business moguls prioritize building long-term relationships with their customers, using techniques such as personalized marketing, loyalty programs, and excellent customer service. This chapter delves into the strategies used to foster customer loyalty and the impact it has on business success.

8

Chapter 8: Customer-Centric Approach

A customer-centric approach is a hallmark of successful businesses. Business moguls prioritize customer satisfaction and loyalty, understanding that happy customers are key to long-term success. This chapter explores the strategies they use to engage with customers, gather feedback, and continuously improve their products and services based on customer needs.

Putting the customer first begins with understanding their needs and expectations. Business moguls conduct thorough market research and use customer feedback to inform their decisions. This chapter delves into the methods used to gather customer insights and how they are integrated into business strategies.

Customer engagement is crucial for building strong relationships. Business moguls use various techniques to connect with their customers, from social media interactions to personalized communications. This chapter explores the importance of engaging with customers and creating positive experiences that foster loyalty.

Continuous improvement is a key aspect of a customer-centric approach. Business moguls are committed to refining their products and services based on customer feedback. This chapter examines the processes used to gather and analyze feedback, as well as the strategies for implementing changes that enhance customer satisfaction.

Customer service plays a vital role in a customer-centric business. Business moguls prioritize providing exceptional customer service, ensuring that their customers feel valued and supported. This chapter delves into the principles of excellent customer service and the impact it has on customer loyalty and retention.

Lastly, this chapter highlights the importance of building a customer-focused culture within the organization. Business moguls create a culture where every employee is committed to delivering value to the customer. This chapter explores the strategies used to foster a customer-centric mindset and the benefits it brings to the business.

9

Chapter 9: Leveraging Technology

In the digital age, leveraging technology is essential for staying competitive. Business moguls embrace technological advancements to streamline operations, enhance productivity, and create new opportunities. This chapter examines how they integrate technology into their business models, stay ahead of technological trends, and use data to make informed decisions.

Technology integration begins with identifying the right tools and platforms that align with business goals. Business moguls evaluate various technologies to determine which ones will provide the most value. This chapter explores the process of selecting and implementing technology solutions, as well as the benefits they bring to the organization.

Automation is a key aspect of leveraging technology. Business moguls use automation to streamline repetitive tasks, reduce human error, and increase efficiency. This chapter examines the various ways automation is used in business operations, from customer service chatbots to automated marketing campaigns.

Data-driven decision-making is another crucial element. Business moguls use data analytics to gain insights into customer behavior, market trends, and operational performance. This chapter delves into the importance of data analysis and how moguls use data to make informed strategic decisions.

Staying ahead of technological trends is essential for maintaining a competitive edge. Business moguls are constantly exploring new technologies and innovations that can enhance their business. This chapter examines the importance of staying informed about emerging technologies and the strategies used to stay ahead of the curve.

Lastly, this chapter highlights the role of cybersecurity in leveraging technology. Business moguls prioritize protecting their data and systems from cyber threats. This chapter explores the principles of cybersecurity and the measures taken to ensure the safety and integrity of business operations.

10

Chapter 10: Ethical Leadership

Ethical leadership is about doing the right thing, even when it's not the easiest path. Business moguls understand the importance of integrity and social responsibility. This chapter delves into the principles of ethical leadership, the impact of corporate social responsibility, and how they build trust and credibility with stakeholders.

Ethical leadership starts with a commitment to integrity and transparency. Business moguls prioritize honesty and openness in their dealings, building trust with employees, customers, and partners. This chapter explores the importance of ethical conduct and the strategies used to promote a culture of integrity.

Corporate social responsibility (CSR) is a key aspect of ethical leadership. Business moguls recognize their role in contributing to the well-being of society and the environment. This chapter examines the various CSR initiatives undertaken by moguls, from sustainable business practices to philanthropic efforts.

Building trust with stakeholders is essential for long-term success. Business moguls understand the importance of maintaining strong relationships with employees, customers, investors, and the community. This chapter explores the strategies used to build and maintain trust, including transparent communication and ethical decision-making.

Ethical leadership also involves leading by example. Business moguls set the tone for their organizations by demonstrating ethical behavior in their actions and decisions. This chapter delves into the importance of leading with integrity and the impact it has on organizational culture.

Lastly, this chapter highlights the significance of ethical leadership in navigating challenges and crises. Business moguls prioritize ethical considerations in their decision-making, even in difficult situations. This chapter examines how ethical leadership guides business moguls in overcoming obstacles and maintaining their reputation.

11

Chapter 11: Global Expansion

Expanding a business globally presents both opportunities and challenges. Business moguls have a keen understanding of international markets and the strategies needed to succeed on a global scale. This chapter explores the factors to consider when entering new markets, the importance of cultural sensitivity, and the strategies for navigating regulatory environments.

Entering new markets requires thorough research and planning. Business moguls conduct extensive market analysis to identify opportunities and assess risks. This chapter examines the process of market research and how moguls use this information to inform their global expansion strategies.

Cultural sensitivity is crucial for success in international markets. Business moguls recognize the importance of understanding and respecting cultural differences. This chapter explores the strategies used to navigate cultural nuances and build strong relationships with local stakeholders.

Regulatory environments vary from country to country, and business moguls must navigate these complexities to ensure compliance. This chapter delves into the regulatory considerations of global expansion, including legal requirements, trade regulations, and intellectual property protection.

Building a global brand is another key aspect of international expansion. Business moguls focus on creating a consistent brand identity while adapting to local markets. This chapter examines the strategies used to build a global brand and the importance of maintaining brand integrity.

Lastly, this chapter highlights the importance of strategic partnerships in global expansion. Business moguls leverage partnerships with local businesses, governments, and organizations to facilitate their entry into new markets. This chapter explores the benefits of strategic partnerships and how they contribute to global success.

12

Chapter 12: Leaving a Legacy

The ultimate goal for many business moguls is to leave a lasting legacy. This chapter reflects on the enduring impact of their work, the importance of succession planning, and how they inspire the next generation of leaders. It also highlights the philanthropic efforts of business moguls and their contributions to society beyond the business world.

Leaving a legacy begins with a commitment to long-term impact. Business moguls focus on building businesses that stand the test of time. This chapter explores the principles of sustainable growth and the strategies used to create lasting value.

Succession planning is a critical aspect of leaving a legacy. Business moguls prioritize identifying and developing future leaders to ensure a smooth transition and continued success. This chapter examines the process of succession planning and the importance of nurturing talent within the organization.

Inspiring the next generation of leaders is another key element. Business moguls serve as mentors and role models, sharing their knowledge and experience to guide aspiring entrepreneurs. This chapter delves into the significance of mentorship and the impact it has on the future of business leadership.

Philanthropy and social contributions are also integral to a mogul's legacy. Business moguls use their resources and influence to give back to society and support causes they are passionate about. This chapter highlights the philanthropic efforts of moguls and the positive impact they have on communities and the world.

Finally, this chapter reflects on the enduring impact of a mogul's work. Business moguls leave a legacy not only through their business achievements but also through their contributions to society and the inspiration they provide to others. This chapter celebrates the lasting legacy of business moguls and the lessons they leave for future generations.

From Silicon Dreams to Concrete Realities: The Strategies of Business Moguls

In "From Silicon Dreams to Concrete Realities: The Strategies of Business Moguls," you'll dive into the lives and minds of the world's most successful entrepreneurs. This book takes you on a journey through their dreams, challenges, and triumphs, showcasing the strategies that turned their visionary ideas into thriving businesses.

From the initial spark of inspiration to building strong teams, navigating financial complexities, and leveraging technology, this book covers it all. You'll discover how these moguls maintain a customer-centric approach, innovate continuously, and expand globally while upholding ethical leadership principles. Each chapter is packed with insights and practical advice, offering a blueprint for aspiring business leaders to follow.

Whether you're an entrepreneur looking to start your own venture or someone fascinated by the stories of business giants, this book provides a comprehensive guide to understanding the mindset and tactics of successful business moguls. Get ready to be inspired, learn from their experiences, and apply their strategies to turn your own dreams into concrete realities.

www.ingramcontent.com/pod-product-compliance
Lightning Source LLC
LaVergne TN
LVHW020743090526
838202LV00057BA/6203